MW00909018

STAYING

HEALTHY

BE POSITIVE

Miriam Moss

CRESTWOOD HOUSE
New York

STAYING HEALTHY

BE POSITIVE
CARE FOR YOUR BODY
EAT WELL
KEEP FIT

Series Editor: Kathryn Smith
Series Designer: Helen White

First published in the United States in 1993 by
Crestwood House
Macmillan Publishing Company
866 Third Avenue
New York, NY 10022

Macmillan Publishing Company is part of the Maxwell
Communication Group of Companies.

First Edition
Printed in Italy by G. Canale & C.S.p.A., Turin
10 9 8 7 6 5 4 3 2 1

Library of Congress Cataloging-in-Publication Data

Moss, Miriam.
    Be positive / Miriam Moss.—1st ed.
      p. cm.—(Staying healthy)
    Includes index.
    Summary: Discusses the role of good mental health in being
healthy, covering such aspects as anxiety, stress management,
and the healing powers of the mind.
    ISBN 0-89686-786-2
    1. Health—Juvenile literature.   2. Mental health—Juvenile
literature.   3. Children—Health and hygiene—Juvenile literature.
4. Stress management—Juvenile literature.   [1. Mental health.
2. Health.]   I. Title.   II. Series.
RA777.M685   1993
613—dc20   92-26717

CONTENTS

BE POSITIVE

◄ OPPOSITE **Find a sport you can enjoy. Regular exercise not only improves physical fitness levels, but also can make you feel more positive and happier about life.**

◄ LEFT **Your brain, which is more complicated than any computer, enables you to learn exciting new skills and adapt to new situations. For example, your brain is responsible for coordinating your body and mind when you learn to ride a bike.**

Healthy mind, healthy body

Total health does not mean just physical fitness. There are plenty of extremely fit people who are depressed or even mentally ill. Being healthy means being physically fit and mentally alert, happy and in tune with yourself.

It is very easy to neglect your mental health. This may be partly because what goes on inside our heads is still a bit of a mystery. The brain is an amazingly complex network of nerve cells. It weighs only 2 percent of your total body weight, yet it uses up 20 percent of your energy. It is a remarkable organ that is more complicated than any computer, holding your memories, thoughts, feelings and emotions. It is where you learn, guess, make decisions and fantasize—and it holds your mind.

A wide range of behavior relating to mental health is acceptable in different cultures. In the past many eccentrics were labeled witches and put to death. Even as recently as the beginning of this century it was not uncommon for unmarried pregnant women to be certified insane and put in mental institutions.

Fit for anything!

Do you exercise vigorously for at least 20 minutes two or three times a week? If not, then it's time to change.

It's very simple—you can choose any activity that makes you feel slightly out of breath—brisk walking, running, jogging, cycling, swimming or low-impact aerobics. You'll be surprised how good exercising makes you feel. This is because chemicals that have a calming effect on the mind are released by the brain during exercise. They also contribute to a strong immune system, which helps to defend the body against infections and disease.

If good health means the combination of a healthy body and a healthy mind, how do we get the balance right? Does it mean that we live our lives in a state of partial health? How can we achieve and maintain a sense of well-being? This book deals with these and other questions. It discusses how to preserve your psychological health, giving practical tips on how to cope with and adapt to the stresses of everyday living.

Food for thought

Before dealing with keeping your mind healthy, you need to make sure that your body has every chance of staying fit and well. A healthy, balanced diet is essential for a positive outlook and a healthy body. Poor eating habits and addictions to caffeine, sugar, alcohol or smoking work against your health.

For a balanced diet

- Eat plenty of fresh fruit and raw vegetables, which are full of vitamins and minerals.
- Eat two or three pieces of fruit, a portion of cooked vegetables and a salad every day.
- Eat plenty of fiber for healthy digestion: include brown rice, whole-grain cereals and breads, oats and oat bran in your daily diet.
- Eat cheese, yogurt, fish, legumes (beans, peas and lentils) and meat for protein: Cut down on animal fats by eating less red meat, more fish and using low-fat cheeses.
- Avoid caffeine: Limit the amount of tea, coffee, soft drinks and chocolate you consume.
- Choose foods low in fat, salt and sugar.

◀ OPPOSITE An inactive lifestyle can lead to an inactive mind. Going out and using your time constructively can make you feel far more alert and positive about life.

◀ LEFT Regular exercise keeps your heart and lungs in good condition.

▼ BELOW It's perfectly normal to feel miserable or depressed sometimes. You don't have to feel guilty about it.

Thinking about a change?
Life can sometimes be too hectic for you to manage your mood and look after your body. Negative attitudes, stress and anxiety are all things that directly affect your physical health. You may already feel that you need to take more control of your life by developing a more positive attitude. Try examining your lifestyle, your physical health and your self-image. Do you feel you need to change anything? If so, are you changing for the right reasons? Start by setting yourself some goals. Make sure that they are realistic so that you can ensure success. Look at whether you will need help in achieving your goals. Is the help or support you need available?

YOUR MIND AT REST

Sleep

Sleep is as important to your health as regular exercise and a balanced diet. When you are awake the demands you make on your body are nonstop. Your body can only recover from the day's continuous activity through sleep. Sleep gives you a period of rest in which to grow and repair body tissues. You need at least eight hours every night. A lack of sleep affects your ability to concentrate and leaves you tired and irritable. The effects of poor sleep can build up over several days, so if you stay out late try to go to bed early the next night.

▶ RIGHT **If you find it difficult to relax or go to sleep there is a wide variety of natural herbal teas and remedies, which don't contain caffeine, that can help you to unwind.**

◀ LEFT **The occasional late night is fine, but make sure that you catch up on lost sleep.**

Think of your body as a battery that needs recharging with sleep to function properly.

When you are asleep your heart rate slows down and your body temperature drops. Your breathing becomes shallower and every organ seems to go into neutral. All day long your brain has been absorbing, sifting, analyzing and channeling information. Scientists believe that dreaming is your brain's method of clearing and sorting thoughts and ideas for the next day. By monitoring brain waves during sleep we know that the brain takes several periods of rest in between dreaming. The dreams are a few minutes long and grow in length as the night progresses. People who are constantly awakened during dreaming sleep become very nervous and disturbed after a few weeks. Insomnia—the inability to sleep—can become a serious problem. It is caused by anxiety, overexcitement and even a fear of not being able to sleep.

Everybody experiences problems getting to sleep now and then, but insomniacs may need help from their doctors to overcome the problem.

I s relaxation a luxury?

As well as regular sleep you need to have periods of rest and relaxation during the day. Many people are completely unaware of

I f you want the quickest way to a refreshing night's sleep, try these five tactics:

- Exercise during the evening to help your muscles relax.
- Avoid meals late at night; otherwise your digestive system can't rest while you sleep.
- A warm bath and a hot, milky drink or herbal tea often help to relax you. But avoid drinks containing the stimulant caffeine.
- Make sure you are warm in bed but leave a window slightly open for fresh air.
- Stop working an hour before you go to bed to calm your mind down. If you find that you still cannot sleep, don't lie there tossing and turning: Switch on the light and read.

▼ BELOW **Coffee and tea contain the stimulant caffeine.** **Be aware of how much tea and coffee you drink each day.**

the buildup of tension in their bodies. If you feel anxious or worried about something, you are bound to be tense even if you are not aware of it. This can make you feel very tired, so stay alert to tension and find time to relax. One easy way to relax is to breathe deeply and slowly several times. This is an ideal way to calm down before a test or an exam.

When you feel tension building up, spend a few minutes lying on your bed or on the floor, tensing and relaxing each of the different muscle groups in your body. Work from your toes up to your head and concentrate on feeling your whole body unwind.

Loosen up!

Another way to unwind your mind and muscles is to try out some of the following relaxation exercises.

▶ RIGHT
Shoulders and upper back

Sit straight facing forward with your shoulders down. Breathing in, lift your shoulders up as high and as slowly as you can toward your ears. Then, as you breathe out, roll them back and down, pulling them back as far as possible in a circular movement.

◀ LEFT
Lower back

Sit comfortably and clasp your hands behind the back of your head. Let your elbows fall forward, draw in your chin and lower your head until you can feel the muscles in your neck stretch.

▼ BELOW **Neck and shoulders**

Lie on your stomach on the floor with your hands meeting in front of your body and your elbows flat out on the floor. Raise your head slowly and then, keeping your head back, push up gently. Go as high as is comfortable and hold for a count of five; then lower yourself to the floor.

TROUBLED MINDS

Anxiety

Mental illness is as widespread as cancer but is still widely misunderstood. Everyone feels worried or anxious sometimes, but if your anxiety becomes intense and prolonged, and everything seems threatening, then it can lead to depression and other illnesses. Severe anxiety means being in a state of constant worry. This may be caused by a traumatic event, an illness or a long period of stress. Sometimes severe anxiety is followed by panic attacks, which can be strong enough to stop a person from being able to leave his or her own home.

Neurosis

Anxiety can lead to neuroses, which can become obsessional. The simplest form of obsessional neurosis is continually checking that your front door is locked, even when you know it is. One of the most common forms of obsessional behavior is an obsession with cleanliness.

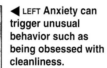
◀ LEFT Anxiety can trigger unusual behavior such as being obsessed with cleanliness.

▶ OPPOSITE Being happy with yourself shows in your appearance, body language and energy level. See if you can tell whether someone is feeling low and depressed or positive and energetic.

easily treated disorders. Phobics are gently faced with their fear and through familiarity, over a period of time, they manage to control their anxiety.

Depression

Depression covers a wide range of thoughts and feelings from sadness to complete hopelessness. Depression is usually short-lived and life regains its color and interest once again. But for some it becomes established, lasting for months. The sufferer then needs to seek professional treatment because he or she is too locked into the depression to be objective. Signs of depression may be a lack of energy, a slowing down of thoughts and movements, a significant increase or decrease in weight, sleep problems and a loss of interest in activities once enjoyed.

Depression is a recognized illness that can be treated in a number of ways. Milder depressions can be treated by discussing what is upsetting you. Counseling goes further by identifying difficulties and encouraging you to take practical steps to deal with them. There are many counseling services, including your doctor, social worker or psychiatrist. With a psychiatrist you examine your personal conflicts and self-doubts over a number of months, either alone or in a group. Anti-depressant drugs are given in many cases of depression. These are used when the depression is "biological," caused by chemical or genetic factors.

Hours a day may be spent washing hands to get rid of any speck of dirt. If something dirty is accidentally touched, then the whole washing ritual is repeated.

Phobias

A phobia is an acute anxiety that is attached to particular objects, animals or situations. This could be a fear of frogs blown out of proportion, leading to real feelings of panic.

Many people are agoraphobics, who fear open spaces. These fears often become stronger during periods of stress. Other people are social phobics, who get panic attacks in crowds or shopping malls. Often this phobia starts in teenagers and improves with time, sometimes without treatment.

Phobias are among the most

◄ OPPOSITE
Depression is a recognized illness that can be treated. If you can't shake off a depression over a long period of time you need to seek professional help.

► RIGHT It's very easy to feel isolated by depression and to think when you look around that everyone else is happier than you are. In any crowd of people some will be suffering and unhappy. Focusing on this sometimes helps to put your own problems into perspective.

STRESS MANAGEMENT

▲ ABOVE **One way to combat stress is by taking up a new sport.**

◀ **Certain levels of stress can enhance performance. But there comes a point when the body and mind become overloaded. It's vital that you learn to recognize the signs, and manage your stress.**

Creating stress

Stress can be caused by anything from stubbing your toe to the death of someone close to you. When you feel anger, frustration, fear or anxiety your body sends out hormones, such as adrenaline, to put your body on red alert, preparing it for fighting or running away from the situation. Reacting like this over and over again causes stress. A buildup of these hormones leads to tension and fatigue.

Out of control?

We are unable to control certain stressful events that are outside ordinary experience. Traumas such as bereavement or being in a major accident sometimes result in post-traumatic stress disorders. Sufferers lose interest in aspects of their lives. They feel detached from others and often find it hard to express their emotions or talk about their feelings. Sometimes we can control the amount of stress we are exposed to by making sensible, everyday decisions, such as not taking on too much responsibility and preparing ourselves better to avoid panic. However, because too little stress can make life seem uneventful and boring, many people create their own stress. Certain levels of stress are stimulating, challenging and good for you. Think of the athlete who needs to get "psyched up" before a race. As stress increases so does your performance and efficiency—up to a point.

Having learned how to recognize the signs of stress, you need to gauge the level of stress that is your own personal limit. Then you need to find efficient, practical ways of relieving stress. One way of dealing with unwanted levels of stress is to remove the source. Work out the cause of your anxiety. Can you avoid it by changing your attitude toward it? Would it help to talk to a friend about it?

The effects of stress

Too much stress will put your mental and physical health under threat. The effects on your body are many. For example, stress tends to accelerate skin problems such as eczema, acne or psoriasis because skin acts as a screen where physical and psychological disorders show themselves. Stress can cause anxiety, depression, loss of concentration and loss of memory. Headaches, insomnia and other sleep disorders are linked to stress. Asthma becomes worse with stress and it may also affect the immune system. Many stomach upsets, such as ulcers and an

◀ This child is suffering from eczema, which can be a stress-related skin disorder. Sometimes it can be helped by a number of natural remedies, including specially prescribed diets.

irritable colon, as well as pulse-rate changes and palpitations, are also linked to stress. Stress often leads to muscle tension, resulting in aches and pains, especially in the neck and shoulders. Mouth ulcers and cold sores, increased hair loss, loss of periods in girls and impotence in boys can accompany long periods of stress.

The straw that broke the camel's back

People deal with stress in different ways. One person's stimulation may be another person's breaking point. Some people thrive on stress while others can only cope with a little. At some point we all begin to suffer from overload and, if the pressure continues, lose our ability to cope, become exhausted and finally ill.

Coping with stress is something everybody has to do, but first you have to be able to recognize when you are stressed. Under stress your heart beats faster and your blood pressure may rise. Extra blood is sent to your muscle groups, more sugar is released into the blood for energy and your breathing becomes faster and deeper for added oxygen. Your temperature also rises and you sweat more to control it. All these changes help you cope with any action you may need to take while under pressure.

Taking charge

How do you avoid unwanted levels of stress? First of all it's up to you. No one else can give you a less stressful life! A few minor lifestyle changes can do the trick. Here are a few tips to help you take control.

● To get organized, make a list of all the things you need to do.

● Be realistic about perfection—you're only human. Being kind to yourself means accepting your own circumstances for what they are. It's a real waste of time to constantly compare yourself unfavorably with others. (There will always be someone you can't match up to in one way or another.)

● Compulsive worriers should set

◀ After a difficult day, releasing stress is essential. One good way is to play a really energetic sport that leaves you relaxed and refreshed.

▼ Successful studying means organizing your workload and giving yourself time off to relax and enjoy yourself.

aside a time each day for worry. This prevents these thoughts from taking over the rest of the day.

● Make sure you have an active lifestyle. Exercise keeps you healthy and relaxes you.

Surviving schoolwork

No one says it's easy spending long days at school and working hard in the evening to get homework finished on time (never mind fitting in your social life as well). Successful studying takes determination and guts. Sometimes you may wonder whether it's worth the trouble, especially with the added stress of exams. Everyone feels depressed sometimes about work, school or the future. Talking to friends who are in the same boat usually helps to ease negative feelings. Certainly there is no point worrying or working yourself so hard that you become ill. If you feel that it's all too much, then analyze your day and see how you can change it.

Take pleasure in crossing things off as you go along, but don't expect to do everything in one day. Your list will stop you from worrying that somehow, somewhere, you have forgotten to do something important.

● Learn to say no occasionally. When you start to feel under pressure, give up one or two activities that are not essential.

● Know when you are tired. Then make sure you get enough sleep to recharge your batteries.

● Eat well and avoid nicotine, alcohol and stimulants such as caffeine.

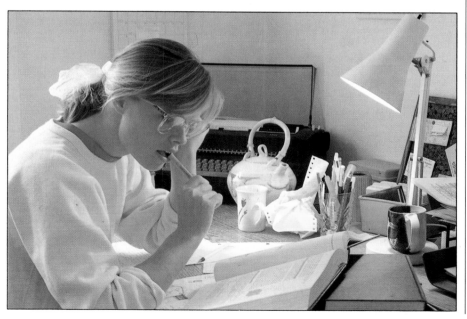

◀ If you feel depressed already, the best way to feel worse is to drink alcohol, which is a depressant.

▶ Talking over a problem with friends is one of the best ways of sorting it out.

successful treatments in psychiatry. It's a great way to relieve tension and deal with negative emotions. If, however, you think you need professional help then try talking to your doctor, who may refer you to a counselor or therapist. There is information about this to help you on p. 31.

Are you giving yourself enough time off in which to relax? Organize your deadlines so that they are more realistic. Break down chunks of work into smaller sections and cross them off on a list as you go. This encourages you and gives you a sense of achievement. Stop once you've reached your goal and enjoy yourself!

Talking about it

If you are feeling stressed and want to reduce the effects, one tried-and-tested method is to talk over a problem with someone you can trust. This often takes the sting out of a situation. No one really knows why it works, but it is one of the oldest and most

When things go wrong

Sometimes people turn to unprescribed drugs or alcohol because they are feeling depressed. If you are feeling miserable, alcohol, which is a depressant, will make you feel worse by exaggerating your mood. It is a very powerful poison that affects every cell in your body, especially those in the liver, heart and brain. Turning to alcohol doesn't solve problems; it creates them. The story is the same with many illegal drugs. They may make you feel better for a short time, but the low that follows the high will probably make you feel worse than you did before.

In the long run, as the highs lose their strength, you will have to keep taking the drug just to feel "normal." By this time trying to stop probably will make you feel very ill.

What are friends for?

Your friends are very important when you are trying to deal with stress. Not only can they help by listening to you, but friendships can also help you feel positive about yourself and are good for self-esteem. Friends come in all shapes and sizes. You have to accept them for what they are because it's all about giving and taking. How good a friend do you make? Try yourself out on this list:

• Are you...

someone to confide in?

someone who will tell the truth?

someone to share jokes with?

someone whose opinion is valuable?

someone who is generous toward others and makes them feel good?

someone who can be relied on?

someone who will speak up when something seems wrong?

someone who sticks up for others?

Being part of a group is also important, especially to teenagers who are trying to find their own identities. Groups often form around shared interests. These may be similarities in what you wear, how you talk, what you own, what you do or where you spend your time. You can sort out your own identity through the group's. In a group your problems and pleasures can be shared and you can find loyalty and trust.

◀ LEFT
Communicating with others is one of your most important skills. It avoids misunderstandings and helps you to get the most out of your relationships.

▲ ABOVE Having a hobby or an interest in which you can become really involved can help you to sort out your own identity.

THE HEALING TOUCH

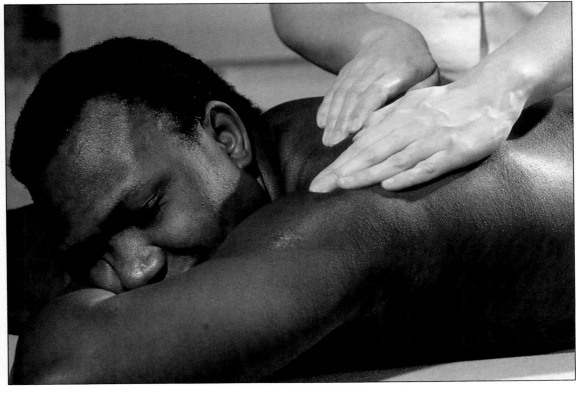

▲ ABOVE
A professional aromatherapy masseuse uses aromatic oils to relax the body and give a sense of well-being.

◀ LEFT More and more people are turning to natural remedies, some of which have been tried and tested over thousands of years.

Good for the mind

There are numerous activities that you can choose to keep yourself positive and relaxed. Many are aimed at relieving stress, all of them are good for the mind, and most are extremely enjoyable!

The marvels of massage

The age-old art of massage is soothing and relaxing for both receiver and giver. Massage removes stress and improves self-image. Equip yourself with some massage oil and a few basic massage strokes from a book. Give your friend a half-hour treat by massaging the aches and tension knots from the shoulders and neck. Get your friend to sit on a chair or lie on a firm surface. For a truly relaxing massage make sure you have a warm, peaceful room. Aromatherapy, massage using scented oils, is a great treat for the senses. Try using a few drops of orange, mandarin or sandalwood oil for a relaxing and aromatic massage.

Yoga

Yoga is a gentle activity that relaxes the mind and body and results in a sense of well-being. There are some specific yoga poses to calm nerves and cure sleep problems. Here are two poses to calm you down.

a. The pose of tranquility

Lying on your back, stretch your arms over your head. Bring your legs and arms up straight to meet each other just overhead. Rest your legs on the palms of your hands so that your legs, body and arms form a triangle. Hold the position as long as it is comfortable and breathe deeply.

b. The pose of a dead person

Lie on your back with your feet together, arms by your sides and your eyes closed. Relax your muscles from the toes upward while breathing quietly and rhythmically. Slowly deepen your breathing and take your mind away from your surroundings.

▼ The pose of a dead person is particularly useful to those who have problems going to sleep.

▲ The pose of tranquility is designed to calm the nerves. Rest the weight of your legs on the upturned palms of your hands to achieve a balanced position.

Acupuncture

Acupuncture is an ancient art that has been used by the Chinese for thousands of years. It is effective in treating hundreds of illnesses, and it can kill pain. Acupuncture treatment takes the body, the mind and the external environment of the sufferer into consideration. Treating the whole person is called the holistic approach, which means "of the whole." Treatment changes according to the patient's changing physical and mental condition. Acupuncture divides the body into meridian lines, or lines of energy, where the acupuncturist inserts very fine needles to stimulate the nerves and relieve blockages in the body's energy flow. This cures a range of conditions from broken limbs to depression. If you are squeamish about needles, the same meridian lines are used in acupressure, in which pressure is used instead of needles.

Winding down

Doing something different after a hard day's work helps you to wind down. You can choose from a wide variety of activities. Many people enjoy juggling. The physical exercise and the concentration involved help to disperse stress. It is fun, healthy and leaves you with a sense of calm and well-being. People have their own preferences when it comes to relaxing. Some people enjoy reading, knitting or playing chess; others couldn't live without their stereo or television. Some find that more physical activities, such as going for a bike ride,

hiking, kicking a ball around or playing squash, are excellent ways of winding down.

Calming down—naturally

Can old remedies really relieve stress? At least 200 plants are said to have stress-relieving properties. Some help calm you down if you are agitated or in pain. Oil of cloves, for example, is effective for relieving a toothache. Pillows made out of hops are said to help you sleep peacefully. The plant feverfew is used to relieve migraines and tension head-aches. Lemon balm is used to calm small children, and lime blossom is recommended for stressed adults and hyperactive children. Ginseng is a general health tonic that stimulates the whole body and helps protect against the long-term effects of stress.

An increasing number of people use flower remedies. These are recommended to help with certain unwanted feelings: Rock rose is for fear; olive for exhaustion; impatiens for impatience and a combined rescue remedy for general stress and trauma.

▲ ABOVE **Are you good at recognizing the signs of a build-up of tension? Do you give yourself enough time to relax?**

◀ LEFT **Camomile is used in a number of preparations because of its relaxing properties. These include herbal teas and soothing creams.**

ALL IN THE MIND?

Hidden depths

Our brains play a major part in keeping us healthy, but we know very little about how they work. Psychology, the study of the mind, comes from the Greek words psyche (soul) and logos (wisdom or knowledge). As we use a very small percentage of our brains in everyday life, the potential of our brains and minds remains relatively unexplored. Our minds are like icebergs—a tiny part shows as our "conscious" thoughts, but most thoughts and feelings are hidden in our "subconscious."

Mind over matter?

More attention is being paid to relaxation techniques that help strengthen our ability to resist disease by improving mental well-being. There is a growing interest in harnessing the mind to heal the body. Already hypnosis and meditation are used to cure a number of ailments. But is it really possible to heal ourselves of physical and mental disorders by thinking ourselves well? Scientists have tested this by giving half the patients in a group of sufferers a real drug and the other half a placebo—a harmless substitute for the drug. No one knows who has the drug until the end of the test. Surprisingly, in the placebo group, quite a large number are also cured because they *believe* they are taking real medicine. Through experiments like these, doctors are beginning to see how using mind power can help fight disease. A person's attitude toward his or her illness has been proved to have a direct effect on recovery. There are many cases in which a positive attitude toward a life-threatening disease, such as cancer, helps to fight the disease.

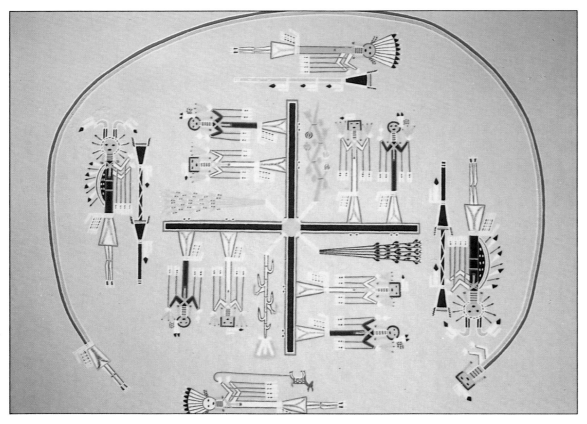

▶ OPPOSITE **Some people believe in the power of creative visualization techniques. For example, some people feel helped by imagining that they can tie their problems to a kite and then let the kite fly away.**

◀ **This sand picture was done by a Navajo healer.**

This is not a new idea. Navajo healers have been treating physical and mental problems without modern drugs for hundreds of years. Their methods of curing people by dancing and storytelling are very effective. They use hypnosis and plants, which change the patient's mood, to restore harmony between the person and the natural world.

Creative mind power

Try out this test, which shows what a powerful hold your imagination has on your body.

Imagine that you have picked up a wedge of lemon and sucked it. You will probably find that your mouth salivates and you might wince at the sour taste.

The creative power of the imagination has been used by experts in relaxation therapies, hypnotherapy and psychology. They use daydreams as a powerful tool for promoting health, healing and a sense of general well-being. These are sometimes called creative visualization techniques. They teach patients to imagine a desired goal to help them achieve it or to rehearse a difficult meeting in their mind's eye. Sometimes they encourage people to imagine positive feelings—for example, their confidence—as a strong, invisible force field around them.

◀ OPPOSITE **Our minds work in mysterious ways. A specific smell such as lavender, for example, can trigger a flood of memories and their accompanying feelings.**

▶ **Being in control of and taking responsibility for your life, as well as knowing how much you can pack into one day without going under, are very important. Planning your time carefully can be a positive aid to keeping life under control.**

Positive thinking

A lot of problems are the result of our believing that there is no escape from a situation, so we feel helpless and hopeless. There are always alternatives of one kind or another. One positive way of getting your own problems into perspective is to think about other people's. Suddenly yours don't seem so impossible after all.

If you can imagine bad things happening to you, then you can also imagine good things, which means you can choose to be positive. Happiness, after all, is not having what you want, but being content with what you have.

Unexpected stressful events *do* take a toll on our ability to adapt and our attitude to life. But if you take care of yourself, keeping both your mind and body healthy, you'll find you have strong reserves with which to combat life's ups and downs.

GLOSSARY

Addiction   Having to use something because you cannot give it up.

Adrenaline   A hormone produced in the body.

Bereavement   To have something or someone special to you taken away.

Blood pressure   The force with which blood is pumped through your veins.

Caffeine   A stimulant found in tea, coffee, chocolate and soft drinks.

Eccentric   A person with unusual or odd behavior.

Eczema   An itchy skin condition.

Hormone   A chemical substance made by the body to control its functions.

Hyperactive   Overactive.

Hypnosis   Putting a person into a state of semiconsciousness.

Immune system   The system in your body that protects you against disease.

Impotence   When a man is unable to perform sexual intercourse.

Meditation   To think about something deeply.

Neurosis   A mild mental disorder caused by anxiety.

Palpitations   Rapid beats of the heart.

Psoriasis   A skin disease.

Psychiatrist   A person who diagnoses and treats mental disorders.

Therapist   A person who helps to treat mental disorders.

Trauma   A powerful shock that may have long-lasting effects.

BOOKS TO READ

Feeling Down: The Way Back Up by Roxane B. Kunz and Judy H. Swenson (Macmillan, 1986)

Exercise & Fitness by Brian R. Ward (Franklin Watts, 1988)

Mind Body Connection by William Check (Chelsea House, 1990)

Amazing Facts about Your Body by Gyles Brandreth (Doubleday, 1981)

You and Your Fitness and Health by Kate Fraser and Judy Tatchell (Educational Development Corp., 1986)

Health and Feelings by Dorothy Baldwin (Rourke Corp., 1987)

Earl Mindell's Herb Bible by Earl Mindell (Simon & Schuster, 1992)

FURTHER INFORMATION

Self Help Center
1600 Dodge Avenue (Suite S-122)
Evanston, IL 60201
1-800-322-MASH
A clearinghouse for information
on self-help groups

Association for the Advancement of
Psychoanalysis (of the Karen Horney
Psychoanalytic Institute & Center)
329 E. 62nd Street
New York, N.Y. 10021
212-751-2724
Maintains consultation and
referral services. Specializes in
children's needs

American Anorexia/Bulimia
Association
418 East 76th Street
New York, N. Y. 10021
212-734-1114

Children's Emotions Anonymous
P.O. Box 4245
St. Paul, MN 55104-0245
612-647-9712
Twelve-step program information
for children ages 6 to 12

Anxiety Disorders Association of
America
6000 Executive Blvd. (Suite 200)
Rockville, MD 20852
301-231-8368

Childhelp USA
6463 Independence Avenue
Woodland Hills, CA 91370
1-800-4-A-CHILD (child abuse
hot line)

Covenant House Nineline
1-800-999-9999

Al-Anon/Alateen
Family Group Headquarters Inc.
P.O. Box 862
Midtown Station
New York, N.Y. 10018-0862
212-302-7240 (Al-Anon)
1-800-356-9996 (Alateen)

National Council on Alcoholism
and Drug Dependence
12 W. 21st Street
New York, N.Y. 10010
212-206-6770
1-800-475-HOPE

American Association for
Acupuncture and Oriental
Medicine
1424 16th Street NW (Suite 501)
Washington, D.C. 20036
202-265-2287

INDEX

Photo Credits

Action Plus 7 (top); Chapel Studios 9, 10, 12, 29; B. Coleman 27; Eye Ubiquitous 17, 20 (right, L. Fordyce); Jeff Greenberg 8, 28 (bottom); S&R Greenhill 18 (top); Hutchinson 25 (top); Tony Stone 6 (top), 7 (bottom), 15, 16, 19 (L. Adamski Peek), 20 (left, P&K Smith), 21 (bottom, G. Loucel), 22 (M. Busselle), 26; Science Photo Library 23 (top); Zefa 4, 5, 13, 14, 20, 21 (top right), 25 (bottom), 28 (top, J. Flowerdew).
Artwork by Debbie Hinks.